CARING FOR YOUR AGING PARENTS

6 SENSITIVE STUDIES FOR WOMEN WITH FAMILIES IN TRANSITION

DR. JUDY HAMLIN

VICTOR BOOKS®

A DIVISION OF SCRIPTURE PRESS PUBLICATIONS INC.
USA   CANADA   ENGLAND

Scripture quotations are taken from the Holy Bible, New International Version, © *1973, 1978, 1984, International Bible Society. Used by permission of Zondervan Bible Publishers.*

Copyediting: Pamela T. Campbell
Cover Design: Scott Rattray
Cover Illustration: Janet Hamlin
Interior Illustrations: Darrel Skipworth

Recommended Dewey Decimal Classification: 243.833
Suggested Subject Heading: BIBLE STUDY: WOMEN
Library of Congress Catalog Card Number: 92-80119
ISBN: 0-89693-097-1

1   2   3   4   5   6   7   8   9   10 Printing/Year 96   95   94   93   92

VICTOR BOOKS
A division of SP Publications, Inc.
Wheaton, Illinois 60187

CONTENTS

To Knox and Evelyn,
who provided my caregiving opportunities;
and to Joe Ann,
who shared them with me.

INTRODUCTION

Since nearly everyone in our society reaches the age of 65, most women studying this book will have the opportunity to care for an aging family member. Increasingly this care will occur even as children remain at home, compounding the demands on the caregiver's time and complicating the home setting.

Among my age group (40–50), it has not been common to hear stories shared regarding care for an aging family member. Information has been limited not because it was unavailable but due to a lack of research.

After having the blessing of my mother living with my family for nine years following my father's death, then losing her to cancer after my sister and I provided her with continuous care for three months, it is my prayer that we who find ourselves in such God-given circumstances share the ups and downs, highs and lows, blessings and curses, to build up others with love and hope.

Each session includes:

- ☐ *Scripture* and *Purpose* statements reflect the goals of the session.
- ☐ *Looking Inside* combines questions with illustrations to be used as conversation starters.
- ☐ *Topical Text* prompts participants to work through specific issues.
- ☐ *Scriptures* that speak to those specific issues.
- ☐ *Prayer Together* encourages participants to develop the discipline of prayer and praise

In the *Leader's Notes* you will find background information, additional questions, and an outline for each session. During the course of this study the Holy Spirit might prompt you to make a decision to receive Jesus Christ as your Lord and Savior. If this happens, turn to the back of the study and review the Five Steps. You may do this alone, with a friend or with your group leader. Record your spiritual birthday, then read, claim, and receive God's gifts.

You're Not Alone

SCRIPTURE

"But if a widow has children or grandchildren, these should learn first of all to put their religion into practice by caring for their own family and so repaying their parents and grandparents, for this is pleasing to God" *(1 Timothy 5:4).*

PURPOSE

To present current statistics on aging, and help participants gain perspectives on family members' lives.

LOOKING INSIDE

1. What age do you consider "old"?

2. Has your concept of "old" changed during the past 10 years? If yes, why?

3. What one memory stands out regarding the aging of your parents?

STATUS OF OLDER WOMEN[1]

Check True or False next to the following statements.

True	False	
		The over 50 group is growing twice as fast as the U.S. population as a whole.
		The over 50 group has $500 billion worth of spending power.
		People 65 or over will double in number to 51 million by the year 2020.
		Those 85 and older (the fastest-growing group) will make up 5% of the U.S. population by the year 2050.
		About 15 million American women are over the age of 65.
		Some 3.5 million American women are over 80.
		Women 65 and older make up 60% of America's elderly population.
		There are six widows for every widower.
		The average age of widowhood is 56.
		More than half of all women over 65 are widows, and 70% of those over 75 are widows.
		Six out of ten widows live alone.
		There are 857,000 divorced women between the ages of 55 and 64. They make up 7.3% of the population.
		Some 467,000 women, or 5.2 percent of the population, between the ages of 65 and 74 are divorced.
		There are 158,000 divorced women over the age of 75. They comprise 2.6% of the population.
		White women have a life expectancy of 78.5 years (compared to 71.1 years for men).
		Black women have a life expectancy of 73 years (compared to 64.4 years for men).
		One-third of older women depend on Social Security payments for 90% or more of their income.

1. Which of the above statements surprises you most? Why?

---

1. Jane Seskin. *Alone—Not Lonely* (Glenview, Ill: Scott, Foresman and Co., 1985), p. 2.

2. Which statement most impacts your thoughts toward aging? Why?

Turn to your neighbor and discuss a current situation regarding an aging family member.

A BIBLICAL PICTURE OF AGING

Read and reflect on the following passage in Ecclesiastes concerning the aging process. Be prepared to identify times to "remember Him (God, the Creator)."

"Remember your Creator in the days of your youth, before the days of trouble come and the years approach when you will say, 'I find no pleasure in them'—before the sun and the light and the moon and the stars grow dark [the mind], and the clouds return after the rain; when the keepers of the house tremble [the hands], and the strong men stoop [bones], when the grinders cease because they are few [teeth], and those looking through the windows grow dim [eyes]; when the doors to the street are closed [lips] and the sound of grinding fades [hearing]; when men rise up at the sound of birds, but all their songs grow faint; when men are afraid of heights and of dangers in the streets [heart]; when the almond tree blossoms [white hair] and the grasshopper drags himself along [kyphosis] and desire no longer is stirred [sexual function]. Then man goes to his eternal home and mourners go about the streets. Remember him—before the silver cord [spinal cord] is severed, or the golden bowl [brain] is broken" (Ecclesiastes 12:1-6).[2]

What does this biblical picture say to you?

Remember Him:

---

2. Bracketed material from Robert D. Orr, M.D., et al. *Life & Death Decisions: Help in Making Tough Choices About Bioethical Issues* (Colorado Springs, Colo.: NavPress, 1990), pp. 133-34.

Remember Him:

Remember Him:

PRAYING TOGETHER
Select one of the following printed prayers that best fits your need today and pray during the group prayer time.

Father, give me a new awareness of _____'s
feelings and concerns. *(my aging family member)*

Dear Father, thank You for this group and the ability to share my situation.

Lord, show me and guide me in the path I should take regarding
_____ .

Father, give me patience in dealing with _____ .

THIS WEEK
Schedule an informal appointment with your aging family member. Make a point of just listening. Ask only one question: "What is your fondest family memory?"

After the appointment make notes, and bring them to the next session.

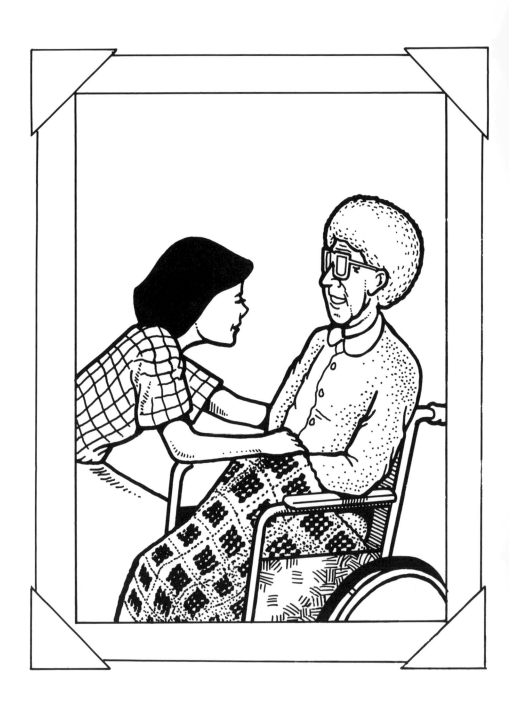

SEARCHING FOR ANSWERS 2

IDENTIFYING CONCERNS

SCRIPTURE
"Near the cross of Jesus stood His mother, His mother's sister, Mary the wife of Clopas, and Mary Magdalene. When Jesus saw His mother there, and the disciple whom He loved standing nearby, He said to His mother, 'Dear woman, here is your son,' and to the disciple, 'Here is your mother.' From that time on, this disciple took her into his home" *(John 19:25-27).*

PURPOSE
To identify concerns about the aging process, and identify solutions.

LOOKING INSIDE
1. What are the most important concerns in your life?

2. Do you aggressively seek solutions to your concerns? Why or why not?

3. Do you feel guilt after you've made decisions?

IDENTIFYING CONCERNS
The following chart lists concerns of people who are dealing with an aging family member. First identify the person for whom you are concerned and write his or her name at the top of the chart. Then, check how concerned you are about each item.

CONCERNS	ALWAYS	OFTEN	SOMETIMES	SELDOM	NOT AT ALL	UNSURE
Health/Health care						
Will to live						
Social life (friends)						
Finances						
Transportation						
Loneliness						
Dealing with grief						
Diet & exercise						
Lifestyle						
Legal advice						
Housing						
Insurance						
Shopping						
Crime rate/safety						
Activities						
Spiritual life						
Family relationships						
Holidays						
Emotional health						
Employment						
Personal hygiene						
Coping						
Ability to make decisions						

List your "Always" concerns:

_____   _____

_____   _____

_____   _____

Select one concern from the "Always" list:

_____

Create a list of factors dealing with the concern:

1. _____

2. _____

3. _____

4. _____

5. _____

Pair off with someone in the group who shares a similar concern. Together, attempt to create a resource list.

_____

_____

_____

_____

_____

_____

AGING BIBLICAL CHARACTERS

A partial solution to dealing with an aging family member may involve an assessment and evaluation of oneself. Do we have a need to grow up and begin accepting the aging process for ourselves? It might require restructuring our values, lifestyles and priorities. Several biblical characters faced difficulties with life transitions. See if you identify with any of the following characters' actions.

David

"In the spring, at the time when kings go off to war, David sent Joab out with the king's men and the whole Israelite army. They destroyed the Ammonites and besieged Rabbah. But David remained in Jerusalem. One evening David got up from his bed and walked around on the roof of the palace. From the roof he saw a woman bathing. The woman was very beautiful, and David sent someone to find out about her. The man said, 'Isn't this Bathsheba, the daughter of Eliam and the wife of Uriah the Hittite?' Then David sent messengers to get her. She came to him, and he slept with her. (She had purified herself from her uncleanness.) Then she went back home" *(2 Samuel 11:1-4).*

Martha

"As Jesus and His disciples were on their way, He came to a village where a woman named Martha opened her home to Him. She had a sister called Mary, who sat at the Lord's feet listening to what He said. But Martha was distracted by all the preparations that had to be made. She came to Him and asked, 'Lord, don't You care that my sister has left me to do the work by myself? Tell her to help me!' " *(Luke 10:38-40)*

Moses

"Now Moses was tending the flock of Jethro his father-in-law, the priest of Midian, and he led the flock to the far side of the desert and came to Horeb, the mountain of God. . . . The Lord said, 'I have indeed seen the misery of My people in Egypt. I have heard them crying out because of their slave drivers, and I am concerned about their suffering. . . . So now, go. I am sending you to Pharaoh to bring My people the Israelites out of Egypt' " *(Exodus 3:1, 7, 10)*.

Jonah

"The word of the Lord came to Jonah son of Amittai: 'Go to the great city of Nineveh and preach against it, because its wickedness has come up before me.' But Jonah ran away from the Lord and headed for Tarshish. He went down to Joppa, where he found a ship bound for that port. After paying the fare, he went aboard and sailed for Tarshish to flee from the Lord" *(Jonah 1:1-3)*.

"Then they took Jonah and threw him overboard, and the raging sea grew calm. At this the men greatly feared the Lord, and they offered a sacrifice to the Lord and made vows to Him. But the Lord provided a great fish to swallow Jonah, and Jonah was inside the fish three days and three nights" *(Jonah 1:15-17)*.

PRAYING TOGETHER

Choose the prayer pattern that best fits your need today, fill in the blank(s) and pray during the group prayer time. Let the designated leader close the prayer time.

Father, I pray for wisdom and discernment regarding family decisions.

Lord, make me bold in my task of caring for_____ .

Build my confidence and trust in Your provisions.

Father, show me the way to evaluate my priorities and make Your will my will.

THIS WEEK

This week continue to work on your resource list on the main identified concern. The Appendix will help you begin your search. Next week you will share information with your partner.

SEARCHING FOR ANSWERS

3

"HOW TO" HELP

SCRIPTURE
"Therefore do not worry about tomorrow, for tomorrow will worry about itself. Each day has enough trouble of its own" *(Matthew 6:34)*.

PURPOSE
To provide insights for helping your aging parents deal with daily routines.

LOOKING INSIDE
1. Describe the last discussion you had with one of your parents. Did you listen attentively?

2. How often do you call or visit your parent(s)?

3. Do you encourage your parent(s) to make their own decisions . . .

> all the time?
> sometimes?
> seldom?
> never?

RECOGNIZING WHEN HELP IS NEEDED
Physical losses occur at different times as one ages. It is generally around age 70 when a person begins to feel physically limited.

By being aware of the losses we can "help."

Loss of vision

Loss of hearing

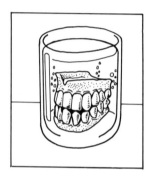

Loss of teeth

Loss of balance

Loss of taste

Loss of smell

Loss of strength

Slow reaction time

Less effective kidneys

Less elastic bladder

Less effective lungs and heart

Constricted digestion

The above losses do not incapacitate older people. Most losses can be compensated for. However, when an older person encounters a circumstance such as a car accident, he or she experiences greater stress than a younger person might face. Anger and depression may accompany the event due to a feeling of foolishness or having made a mistake. It is vital for the aging person to be in a comfortable, secure environment, in which he or she is encouraged and loved.

"The Lord God said, 'It is not good for the man to be alone' "
(Genesis 2:18).

THE BIBLE AND OLD AGE

Read the following Scriptures underlining key words and phrases
that identify physical changes due to aging and instruction on
how people who are aging should be treated.

"When Isaac was old and his eyes were so weak that he could
no longer see, he called for Esau his older son and said to him,
'My son.' 'Here I am,' he answered" *(Genesis 27:1).*

"Honor your father and your mother, so that you may live long in
the land the Lord your God is giving you" *(Exodus 20:12).*

"Rise in the presence of the aged, show respect for the elderly
and revere your God. I am the Lord" *(Leviticus 19:32).*

"One night Eli, whose eyes were becoming so weak that he
could barely see, was lying down in his usual place" *(1 Samuel
3:2).*

"I am now eighty years old. Can I tell the difference between
what is good and what is not? Can your servant taste what he
eats and drinks? Can I still hear the voices of men and women
singers? Why should your servant be an added burden to my
lord the king?" *(2 Samuel 19:35)*

"When King David was old and well advanced in years, he could
not keep warm even when they put covers over him. So his
servants said to him, 'Let us look for a young virgin to attend the
king and take care of him. She can lie beside him so that our
lord the king may keep warm.' Then they searched throughout
Israel for a beautiful girl and found Abishag, a Shunammite, and
brought her to the king. The girl was very beautiful; she took
care of the king and waited on him, but the king had no intimate
relations with her" *(1 Kings 1:1-4).*

"So Jeroboam's wife did what he said and went to Ahijah's
house in Shiloh. Now Ahijah could not see; his sight was gone
because of his age" *(1 Kings 14:4).*

"He silences the lips of trusted advisers and takes away the discernment of elders" *(Job 12:20).*

"The gray-haired and the aged are on our side, men even older than your father" *(Job 15:10).*

"I thought, 'Age should speak; advanced years should teach wisdom' " *(Job 32:7).*

What do aging people want and need?

1. _____

2. _____

3. _____

4. _____

5. _____

6. _____

7. _____

PRACTICAL HELP
Brainstorm a list of activities for aging family members that include time with family, friends, part-time work or volunteer opportunities.

_____

_____

Create a list of "emergency" numbers and post by all telephones.

_____

_____

PRAYING TOGETHER

Choose the prayer pattern that best fits your need today, fill in the blank(s), and pray during the group prayer time. Let the designated leader close the prayer time.

Father, forgive me for worrying about tomorrow.

Dear Father, give me a keen awareness of physical changes in
_____ .

Lord, increase my awareness of the needs of older people.

Father, help me spend the time to organize _____'s *affairs.*

Dear Lord, help me rest knowing You make all things work for good in my life and with those I love.

THIS WEEK

Gather ideas of possible activities for aging family members, including location, hours, map, etc. Record each idea on a note card, and give one or two ideas to your aging family member this week.

EMOTIONAL SUPPORT

SCRIPTURE
"Rise in the presence of the aged, show respect for the elderly and revere your God. I am the Lord" *(Leviticus 19:32)*.

PURPOSE
To discuss areas of frustration regarding our aging family member which require emotional support.

LOOKING INSIDE
1. Which emotion best illustrates your feeling toward your parents?

2. Share one situation or decision regarding a parent which you have recently faced.

3. Describe the last time you were angry with your parents.

EVALUATE YOURSELF AND YOUR AGING PARENT
Place a yes, no, or question mark in each blank to describe yourself and your aging family member's characteristics.

CHARACTERISTICS	SELF	AGING FAMILY MEMBER
Angers easily		
Adjusts to change easily		
Agrees easily		
Disagrees		
Is frustrated		
Is affirming		
Is manipulative		
Is depressed		
Has guilt feelings		
Is hostile		
Is lonely		
Is a worrier		
Is cheerful		
Has a positive attitude		
Has a negative attitude		

The above evaluation can help you understand older people and their feelings, and help you understand your areas of frustration so you can begin to deal with them.

Identify one area in which you responded no for yourself and yes for your aging family member.

An Example
For example, if you have never been lonely it will be difficult to relate to the aging family member's loneliness. His or her loneliness could result from the loss of a spouse, animal, or the death of a family member or friend.

A Caring Response
Develop a caring response to loneliness. For example:

1. Be an encourager.
2. Try to determine the cause of loneliness.
3. Talk about knowing Jesus.
4. Encourage a quiet time of Bible reading and prayer.
5. Encourage fellowship in a church or small group.
6. Encourage strengthening family relationships.
7. Pray together.

Sharing the Scriptures
Share comforting Scriptures that deal with loneliness.

Depend on God
"Trust in the Lord with all your heart and lean not on your own understanding; in all your ways acknowledge Him, and He will make your paths straight" *(Proverbs 3:5-6).*

Call out to God
"Come to Me, all you who are weary and burdened, and I will give you rest. Take My yoke upon you and learn from Me, for I am gentle and humble in heart, and you will find rest for your souls. For My yoke is easy and My burden is light"
(Matthew 11:28-30).

Obey God
[Teach] "them to obey everything I have commanded you. And surely I am with you always, to the very end of the age"
(Matthew 28:20).

God Will Respond
"God, who has called you into fellowship with His Son Jesus Christ our Lord, is faithful" *(1 Corinthians 1:9).*

We Are Not Alone—Nor Do We Have to Be Lonely
"Keep your lives free from the love of money and be content with what you have, because God has said, 'Never will I leave you; never will I forsake you.' So we say with confidence, 'The Lord is my helper; I will not be afraid. What can man do to me?' " *(Hebrews 13:5-6)*

Remember your area of frustration with your aging family member? Form groups of three and brainstorm some caring approaches to dealing with your chosen topics. Then list some Scriptures concerning those areas.

A Caring Response

Sharing the Scriptures

PRAYING TOGETHER

Choose the prayer pattern that best fits your need today, fill in the blank(s), and pray during the group prayer time. Let the designated leader close the prayer time.

Father, thank You for Your promises and faithfulness.

Dear Father, help me to better understand _____ .

Lord, provide guidance as I seek to encourage and support
_____ .

Father, help me understand causes and effects, and to know what I can do about things.

THIS WEEK
List two things you will do to encourage your aging family member this week.

1. _____

2. _____

ENCOURAGING RELATIONSHIPS

SCRIPTURE

"Do not cast me away when I am old; do not forsake me when my strength is gone" *(Psalm 71:9)*.

PURPOSE

To identify guidelines for relationships with parents as they age.

LOOKING INSIDE

1. How do you feel when people describe something they appreciate about you?

2. Do you often encourage people with whom you have contact?

    all the time   sometimes   seldom   never

3. What one thing would you like for people to say about you in a eulogy?

WAYS TO ENCOURAGE RELATIONSHIPS WITH AGING PARENTS

The following communication exercise, educational opportunities list, and family activities are three ways to encourage relationships.

1. Communication—Talking to and caring for one another, taking the time to listen and ask questions—allows people to share their deepest thoughts. Evaluating communication skills can make people more aware of areas that need improvement. Rank the following on a scale of 1 to 3 (1–needs no improvement, 2–OK, 3–needs improvement).

_____ Amount of listening
_____ Amount of talking
_____ Asking for ideas
_____ Giving feedback
_____ Attentive listening
_____ Guilt feelings
_____ Thinking before speaking
_____ Noting discomfort
_____ Being aware of interest level
_____ Being aware of feelings
_____ Sensing when to avoid certain subjects
_____ Expressing gratitude
_____ Confronting
_____ Voicing anger
_____ Sharing disappointment
_____ Open to help
_____ Criticizing self or others
_____ Talking openly about problems
_____ Amount of time spent
_____ Number of visits
_____ Visiting frequency
_____ Praying for family
_____ Being withdrawn
_____ Asking questions to clarify issues
_____ Demonstrating interest
_____ Voicing praise
_____ Expressing feelings
_____ Being rude
_____ Being warm (loving)
_____ Showing emotions
_____ Hiding emotions
_____ Being withdrawn
_____ Allowing for silence
_____ Being patient
_____ Clarifying intentions

2. Educational Opportunities—Medical research has shown that, barring injury or disease, there's not much change in our brains and our functioning capability between middle age and age 75. Nor do our thinking and reasoning power change much. The fact is "old dogs" can learn new tricks.

"Moses was a hundred and twenty years old when he died, yet his eyes were not weak nor his strength gone" *(Deuteronomy 34:7).*

Educational Opportunities List

_____	_____
_____	_____
_____	_____
_____	_____

3. Family Activities—God honors obedience as we obey His command to honor our father and mother. We are compensated by gaining shared memories, allowing for a time of adjustment before death, and time to say good-bye. The following are a few activities you can do with aging family members.

Look at old photographs and not so old photographs. Talk about each—you will learn a lot about your past.

Ask questions that allow aging parents to talk about their children's experiences, changing occupations through the years, other family members, houses they lived in, their feelings during wars, how they met their spouse, etc.

Realize that each day spent with aging parents could be your last on earth. Place a high value on the time you have together, using it lovingly. If there is any unforgiveness, take care of it—" 'In your anger do not sin': Do not let the sun go down while you are still angry" *(Ephesians 4:26).*

PRAYING TOGETHER
Choose the prayer pattern that best fits your need today, fill in the blank(s), and pray during the group prayer time. Let the designated leader close the prayer time.

Father, thank You for bringing areas to my attention that I need to improve.

Lord, I pray for an openness on behalf of _____ *to sharing time and memories.*

Father, thank You for the time to mend relationships and to prepare to say good-bye to _____ .

Dear Father, I pray for the assignment this week and thank You in advance that each of the three areas will see improvement.

THIS WEEK

From your list of communication skills, list three areas you will work on this week.

1. _____

2. _____

3. _____

Pair off with a friend, agree to call each other once during the week to check on progress toward improvement, and pray for each other.

LOVE ATTACKS (CHILDREN AS CAREGIVERS)

SCRIPTURE

"We love because He first loved us" *(1 John 4:19).*

PURPOSE

To provide methods for self-evaluation and show God's promises for children who care for aging parents.

LOOKING INSIDE

1. How do you feel when someone is kind to you?

2. Who is the first person you trusted? Why?

3. Share one experience in which you gave of yourself to another person.

HOW AM I DOING AS A CAREGIVER?

Be honest about your feelings.

AS A CAREGIVER	GOOD	OK	COULD IMPROVE
Consistent			
Available			
Open			
Accepting			
Positive			
Realistic			
Faithful to trust Jesus			
PHYSICALLY AND OTHER			
Getting enough rest			
Scheduling time wisely			
Proper priorities			
Others help share the load			
Well informed			
Feel appreciated			

Turn to your neighbor and share one area where you are doing "good" and then one area which could be improved.

GOD'S PROMISES FOR THE CAREGIVER

Read the following Scriptures and claim one promise from each.

"The Lord is my shepherd, I shall not be in want" *(Psalm 23:1).*

"Cast your cares on the Lord and He will sustain you; He will never let the righteous fall" *(Psalm 55:22).*

"And we know that in all things God works for the good of those who love Him, who have been called according to His purpose. For those God foreknew He also predestined to be conformed to the likeness of His Son, that He might be the firstborn among many brothers" *(Romans 8:28-29).*

"We are hard pressed on every side, but not crushed; perplexed, but not in despair; . . . Persecuted, but not abandoned; struck down, but not destroyed" *(2 Corinthians 4:8-9).*

"All this is for your benefit, so that the grace that is reaching more and more people may cause thanksgiving to overflow to the glory of God. Therefore we do not lose heart. Though outwardly we are wasting away, yet inwardly we are being renewed day by day. For our light and momentary troubles are achieving for us an eternal glory that far outweighs them all. So we fix our eyes not on what is seen, but on what is unseen. For what is seen is temporary, but what is unseen is eternal" *(2 Corinthians 4:15-18).*

"Do not be anxious about anything, but in everything, by prayer and petition, with thanksgiving, present your requests to God. And the peace of God, which transcends all understanding, will guard your hearts and your minds in Christ Jesus" *(Philippians 4:6-7).*

"I am not saying this because I am in need, for I have learned to be content whatever the circumstances. I know what it is to be in need, and I know what it is to have plenty. I have learned the secret of being content in any and every situation, whether well fed or hungry, whether living in plenty or in want. I can do everything through him who gives me strength" *(Philippians 4:11-13).*

"And my God will meet all your needs according to His glorious riches in Christ Jesus" *(Philippians 4:19).*

"Cast all your anxiety on Him because He cares for you" *(1 Peter 5:7).*

"Blessed are those who mourn, for they will be comforted" *(Matthew 5:4).*

CAREGIVERS MISSION STATEMENT

I am relieved that my calling is to be a caregiver, while God is the curegiver.

I feel a sense of partnership and security, knowing that God is fully present with me and the other person in the caring situation.

I have purpose and direction because I know who motivates me, where I come from, and where I am going.

I feel more competent because I have tools like prayer, Scripture, and blessings.

I feel a sense of inner warmth (and sometimes fear and trembling) when I am privileged to relate to people's deep spiritual needs.

I am free to go the extra mile with those who need me, enhanced by a healthy Christian perspective on servanthood.

I rejoice that the "cups of cold water" I give to others are accepted by God as distinctively Christian caring.

I draw courage from the long line of tradition in which my caring stands, realizing that I actively continue the work carried on by God's people throughout the ages.[1]

PRAYING TOGETHER

Select one or two statements; then, speak the verses with your eyes open.

"The Lord bless you and keep you; the Lord make His face shine upon you and be gracious to you; the Lord turn His face toward you and give you peace" *(Numbers 6:24-26).*

"May the grace of the Lord Jesus Christ, and the love of God, and the fellowship of the Holy Spirit be with you all" *(2 Corinthians 13:14).*

---

1. Reprinted from *Christian Caregiving: A Way of Life* by Kenneth C. Haugk, copyright © 1984 Augsburg Publishing House. Used by permission of Augsburg Fortress.

"And the peace of God, which transcends all understanding, will guard your hearts and your minds in Christ Jesus" *(Philippians 4:7).*

"May God Himself, the God of peace, sanctify you through and through. May your whole spirit, soul and body be kept blameless at the coming of our Lord Jesus Christ. The one who calls you is faithful and He will do it" *(1 Thessalonians 5:23-24).*

"May the God of peace, who through the blood of the eternal covenant brought back from the dead our Lord Jesus, that great Shepherd of the sheep, equip you with everything good for doing His will, and may He work in us what is pleasing to Him, through Jesus Christ, to whom be glory for ever and ever. Amen" *(Hebrews 13:20-21).*

LEADER'S NOTES 1
YOU'RE NOT ALONE

WELCOME
Welcome each woman to the group. Point out to the group that this book includes Scripture, but they may wish to bring their own Bibles. Prayer will be sentence prayers with samples provided. Participation is optional—whenever they feel comfortable, they may pray aloud.

PURPOSE
Have a volunteer read the Scripture and Purpose statement. Discuss the Scripture, sharing from your own personal experience. Stress the fact we're not in this alone, and that statistics in the study will provide new perspectives.

LOOKING INSIDE
Have group members volunteer responses to the three questions. You may need to start the discussion with a personal story.

STATUS OF OLDER WOMEN
Instruct group members to check True or False by each statement concerning the status of older women. Allow four minutes.

After regrouping, reveal the fact that *all* the statements are true. This *is* the future status of older women.

Discuss the two questions. Then have group members turn to their neighbors and discuss a current situation regarding an aging family member. Allow five to six minutes.

A BIBLICAL PICTURE OF AGING
Have volunteers read the Scripture. Instruct group members to highlight key words and phrases. Then ask: **What does this biblical picture say to you?** Possible responses might include:

> Remember Him: In your youth, before physical changes, serve God.

> Remember Him: In days of trouble, a struggle to survive can produce physical changes.

Remember Him: Before death or loss of faculties.

Note that the Scriptures remind us of inevitable physical deterioration and mortality. This passage provides a realistic view of aging, even though many aged people are active and productive.

PRAYING TOGETHER
Take five minutes for prayer. This will vary depending on the group size. The act of prayer may be new for participants, so give them permission not to pray until they feel comfortable. Ask group members to select a printed prayer, then begin prayer time. As leader, it is important for you to pray using only one sentence, modeling the behavior you expect of others.

THIS WEEK
Review the assignment.

LEADER'S NOTES 2
IDENTIFYING CONCERNS

BRIDGE
Ask several members to share their experiences in visiting aging family members. Ask if the question, "What is your fondest family memory?" triggered a response from the aging family member. If not, why?

PURPOSE
Have a volunteer read the Scripture and Purpose statement. Discuss the setting and importance of Jesus entrusting His mother to the disciple and its implications for us.

LOOKING INSIDE
Compile a list of the group's concerns in response to question #1. Continue the discussion, having group members respond to the next questions.

IDENTIFYING CONCERNS
Have a group member read the paragraph describing the chart that lists concerns people face when dealing with aging family members. Have group members record their family member's name at the top of the chart. Allow six to eight minutes to respond to the list, after reviewing the scale.

Instruct group members to list their "Always" concerns. For example: housing, health, lifestyle, coping, etc. Then, have them select one concern from the "Always" list, and record it in the space provided. Brainstorm a list of factors related to the identified concern.

For example, factors related to housing might include:

1. Housing options
2. Family agreement on selected housing option
3. Financial arrangements for housing—who will pay the bills?
4. Medical needs—Does the chosen housing facility offer transportation to the doctor or pharmacy? Is there a nurse at the facility?

5. Privacy for the family and aging family member when he or she lives with the family

Have group members who have similar concerns pair off and create a joint resource list. For example, resources for housing concerns might include the investigation of:

1. Nursing homes
2. Retirement communities
3. Church
4. Specific agencies (American Cancer Society)
5. Home health care

Have several pairs share their work when you reconvene as a large group.

AGING BIBLICAL CHARACTERS
A partial solution to dealing with an aging family member may involve an assessment and evaluation of oneself. Several biblical characters faced difficulties with mid-life transitions. Have volunteers read the Scriptures and see if any group members identify with any of the characters' actions.

David
Point out that David failed to go to work (war) and was tempted. Ask: **Have you ever been disobedient or not done what was right and suffered the consequences?** When it comes to aging parents we need to face situations head-on, making the decisions each day calls for.

Martha
Note that Martha was tired of all the housework and was aggravated. Ask: **Are you sometimes agitated by things like housework, visits to the doctor, or having to talk loud enough for aging ears to hear?** Don't be aggravated. Call out to God for strength and thank Him for the precious time you have with an aging parent. That time will end, and regardless of the level of your responsibilities you will face tears of remorse.

Moses
Moses was being moved from tending sheep to leading people. He was hesitant and asked many questions of God. Ask: **Do you**

question God when you find yourself in situations where the answers don't come easily? Do you hesitate to make decisions you know are best for all concerned? God's response to Moses was "I am who I am. I am all things to you. I will be whatever you need whenever you need it." God is sufficient to meet all our needs.

Jonah

Jonah tried to escape responsibility which led him into his adventure with the great fish. Ask: **Do you try to escape responsibility only to find yourself in a place of deeper quandary?** If you have refused to face your responsibility for an aging parent, leaving the responsibility to others, let Jonah's experience speak to your heart.

Ask: **With which character do you identify the most?** Have group members share any similar situations before they remember one another in prayer.

PRAYING TOGETHER

Take five minutes for prayer. This will vary depending on the size of the group.

THIS WEEK

Make the group aware of the resource list in the Appendix. Encourage them to work on their resource lists and be prepared to share information with their partners at the next session.

LEADER'S NOTES 3
"HOW TO" HELP

BRIDGE

Ask for an update on the search for resources. Who found the most? Take five minutes and have group members share their findings with their partners from the last session.

PURPOSE

Have a volunteer read the Scripture and Purpose statement. Discuss "worrying." Discuss "worrying," pointing out the importance of taking one day at a time. Being prepared to deal with daily routines can help ease worry and concern. Take time as you go through this chapter to laugh, share stories and realize you are not alone.

LOOKING INSIDE

Have group members volunteer responses to the three questions.

RECOGNIZING WHEN HELP IS NEEDED

Review the physical losses listed. Ask if there are others. Have group members place check marks by the losses they have observed in aging parents or family members. Allow time for laughter and funny stories.

Review the paragraph and Genesis 2:18. Ask if anyone can share an experience in which a parent has become depressed or angry due to a stressful event or life change.

THE BIBLE AND OLD AGE

Have volunteers read the Scriptures underlining key words and phrases that identify physical changes due to aging and instruction on how aging people should be treated.

Genesis 27:1	have weak eyes
Exodus 20:12	held in high esteem
Leviticus 19:32	deserve respect

1 Samuel 3:2	have weak eyes
2 Samuel 19:35	loss of taste and hearing
1 Kings 1:4	have poor circulation (can't keep warm)
1 Kings 14:4	loss of sight
Job 12:20	merit trust as wise counsel
Job 15:10	have gray hair
Job 32:7	have wisdom

Have the group brainstorm a list of aging people's wants and needs. After the group has contributed, add others from the following list:

1. Emotional support
2. Security
3. Friends
4. Respect
5. Mental activity
6. Involvement with others
7. Personal independence
8. Self-respect

Tell the group that as we begin to offer help, we need to keep the list of aging peoples' wants and needs in mind.

PRACTICAL HELP

Have the group brainstorm a list of activities for aging family members that include time with family, friends, part-time work or volunteer opportunities. Use the following list if needed:

Travel	Walks	Exercise classes
Golf or tennis	Clubs	Bicycling
Lunch with friends	Movie	Library
Hobbies	Games	Family gatherings
Classes at a college	Church work	Potluck dinners
Community organizations	Crafts	Baby-sitting
Art	Bowling	Reading

Chess   Caregiving
Counseling young people   Bridge
   (parents)

Have the group create a list of "emergency" numbers. Advise group members to post the numbers in several locations. Some of those "emergency" numbers might belong to:

Caregiver   Police
Family member   Fire Department
Doctor   Hospital
Neighbor   Ambulance
Emergency   Pharmacy

PRAYING TOGETHER

Take time for prayer, using the printed prayers or letting people pray for specific aging family members. Close the special time lifting up the caregivers in the group.

THIS WEEK

Review the assignment for the next week.

LEADER'S NOTES 4
EMOTIONAL SUPPORT

BRIDGE
Have volunteers share practical helps or leisure activities they used to encourage their aging family member this past week.

PURPOSE
Have a volunteer read the Scripture and Purpose statement. Help your group work through their frustrations in this session. We often feel we are the only ones who get angry or depressed — we're not. The Scripture should be memorized and recalled whenever needed. God will honor your patience and obedience as you follow His command.

LOOKING INSIDE
Have group members respond to the three questions.

EVALUATE YOURSELF AND YOUR AGING PARENT
Read the instructions for evaluating the characteristics of oneself and the aging parent. Allow three minutes for participants to respond.

Review the example of loneliness, including the ideas for a caring approach and Scriptures which could be shared.

Have group members get in groups of three and discuss caring approaches and ways to overcome the areas they identified in the chart. Then have the groups list Scriptures concerning their topics. You may want to provide each group with a Bible concordance.

As time permits, encourage group members to use the same format to research additional identified areas.

PRAYING TOGETHER
Take about five minutes for prayer. This will vary depending on the size of your group. If you haven't held hands in a circle for prayer, do so at this time.

THIS WEEK

Review the assignment and ask group members to be prepared to report at the next session.

LEADER'S NOTES 5
ENCOURAGING RELATIONSHIPS

BRIDGE
Have group members share their experiences in the two areas they selected to encourage aging family members.

PURPOSE
Have a volunteer read the Scripture and Purpose statement. While encouraging others may not come natural to you, consider the benefits to yourself and to your aging parent. God will bless your obedience in this area.

LOOKING INSIDE
Ask group members if they currently have comfortable relationships with their parent(s) or aging family members. Have group members respond to the three questions.

WAYS TO ENCOURAGE RELATIONSHIPS
Explain that the following communication exercise, educational opportunities list, and family activities are three ways to encourage relationships.

1. Communication—Instruct group members to complete the Communication form, ranking areas that "need improvement," "do not need improvement," or are "OK." Allow four minutes.

Have group members highlight areas that need improvement and record three areas they will work on during the next week on page 36.

2. Educational Opportunities—Read the paragraph on learning capabilities and the aging as well as Deuteronomy 34:7. Then brainstorm a list of educational opportunities. The following are possible responses:

Colleges and Universities	Television Courses
Junior Colleges/Community	Seminaries
Elderhostel	Volunteering
G.E.D. Programs	Church

3. Family Activities—Point out that family activities are ways to build memories. Discuss the two activities listed, then create two more activities (for example: Handling holidays). Close by reading Ephesians 4:26, stressing the importance of having good relationships with aging family members.

PRAYING TOGETHER

Take time for prayer. Remember to give participants permission not to pray. Have the group look at the printed prayers, select one, then begin prayer time. As leader, it is important you pray using one sentence, modeling the behavior you expect of others.

THIS WEEK

Remind each person to work on the three communication skills they have identified as needing improvement. Have group members pair off with a friend, agree to call each other once during the week to check on progress and pray for each other.

LEADER'S NOTES 6
LOVE ATTACKS (CHILDREN AS CAREGIVERS)

BRIDGE
Ask participants to share how well they did this past week in improving weak areas of communication.

PURPOSE
Have a volunteer read the Scripture and Purpose statement. From the Scripture, stress why we care. We care because of God's love for us in sending His son to die on the cross for our sins. Providing a way for each of us to have eternal life. Such love deserves a response on our part. If we accept God's gift of eternal life we also accept His Lordship. God asks us to show respect, to care for, love, and honor the aging. In return, God makes promises to the obedient. Help your group to explore areas in which they may need encouragement and prayer in order to be obedient.

LOOKING INSIDE
Have group members volunteer responses to the three questions.

HOW AM I DOING AS A CAREGIVER?
Have group members rate themselves on how they are doing as caregivers. Instruct group members to pair off and share areas in which they are doing "good" as well as areas which could be improved. Allow six to eight minutes.

GOD'S PROMISES FOR THE CAREGIVER
Have volunteers read each Scripture and highlight or underline promises found in each.

Scripture	Promises
Psalm 23:1	"shall not be in want"
Psalm 55:22	"cast your cares"; "He will sustain you"
Romans 8:28-29	"all things work for the good of those who love Him"
2 Corinthians 4:8-9	"not crushed, not in despair, not abandoned, not destroyed"

2 Corinthians 4:15-18	"inwardly being renewed day by day"; "eternal glory"
Philippians 4:6-7	"the peace of God . . . will guard your hearts and your minds"
Philippians 4:11-13	"be content . . . gives me strength"
Philippians 4:19	"will meet all your needs"
1 Peter 5:7	"He cares for you"
Matthew 5:4	"Be comforted"

Suggest that caregivers memorize these. When times are difficult, being able to recall and claim promises is comforting.

CAREGIVERS MISSION STATEMENT

Review the statement, asking for comments from the group. Suggest that group members may want to clip this statement from their books and place it in their Bibles. Encourage them to read it several times a week and recall situations where God walked with them during the week.

PRAYING TOGETHER

The closing prayer time is a little different this week—we will use benediction Scriptures. Have each person select one or two statements; then, have each one speak her verses with eyes open. Close with the following prayer:

> Now, may God stand below us to support us,
> behind us to push us forward, in front of us
> so that we can see His face and in His face a challenge,
> and above us to watch over and care for us.
> In Jesus' name, Amen.

FOLLOW-UP

This is the last of the six sessions on *Caring for Your Aging Parents*. Select one or more of the following options from the ideas provided, or create your own, allowing your group to fellowship together.

Option 1

If this study ends your time together, plan a fellowship over a potluck meal in about two to three weeks.

Option 2

If you plan to continue meeting as a group, have a fellowship and prayer time at your next meeting; then select the next curriculum you will study.

Option 3

If you're taking a break, assign prayer partners for a weekly telephone check-in, to see how things are going and to pray for expressed needs.

RECORD YOUR CALLS

Members' Need	Date Called	Needed Help	No Help Needed	Prayer Need yes/no

ADDITIONAL RESOURCES

Graham, Billy. *The Billy Graham Christian Worker's Handbook: A Layman's Guide for Soul Winning and Personal Counseling.* Minneapolis, Minnesota: World Wide Publications, 1984.

Gray, Elmer L. *The Bible Answers Senior Adults' Questions.* Nashville, Tennessee: Broadman Press, 1991.

Haugk, Kenneth C. *Christian Caregiving: A Way of Life.* Minneapolis: Augsburg, 1984.

Hauk, Gary. *Building Bonds Between Adults and Their Aging Parents.* Nashville, Tennessee: Convention Press, 1987.

Hawse, III, William L. et al. *Achieving Wholeness in Later Life.* Nashville, Tennessee: Convention Press, 1987.

Jensen, Maxine Dowd. *Old Is Older Than Me and Other Devotionals for the Best Years of Your Life.* San Bernardino, California: Here's Life Publishers, Inc., 1991.

Orr, M.D., Robert D. et al. *Life and Death Decisions: Help in Making Tough Choices About Bioethical Issues.* Colorado Springs, Colorado: NavPress, 1990.

Seskin, Jane. *Alone—Not Lonely: Independent Living for Women Over Fifty.* Washington, D.C.: American Association of Retired Persons, 1985.

Stafford, Tim. *As Our Years Increase.* Grand Rapids, Michigan: Zondervan, 1989.

APPENDIX

POSSIBLE SUPPORT SERVICES
AARP—American Association of Retired People
Adult Day Care Centers
Alzheimer's Association
American Cancer Society
Church Assistance
Crisis Emergency Telephone System
Handyman Programs
Hospital Seminars
Housecleaning Services
Legal Services
Meals on Wheels
Medicare and Medicaid
Nurses Services
Referral Services
SCORE—Service Corps of Retired Executives
Senior Centers
Shopping Services
Silver Yellow Pages
Transportation Services
Yard Services

WHERE TO SEARCH IN THE YELLOW PAGES
American Red Cross
Catholic Charities Family and Community Service
Commission on Aging
Council on Aging
Community Service Society
Department of Community Service
Department of Health
Department of Housing and Community Development
Department of Human Resources
Department of Social Services
Department of Welfare
Family Service Agency
Health and Welfare Agencies
Home Health Care
Homes—Residential Care
Jewish Family and Community Services
Legal Aid

Mental Health Association
Nursing Homes
Nursing Services
Protestant Federation of Welfare Agencies
Retirement and Life Care Communities
Salvation Army
Senior Citizens' Service Organizations
Social Service Agencies
Social Workers
Volunteers of America

FIVE STEPS FOR ACCEPTING JESUS CHRIST AS YOUR PERSONAL LORD AND SAVIOR

"For God so loved the world, that He gave His one and only Son, that whoever believes in Him shall not perish but have eternal life" *(John 3:16)*

ACTION	SCRIPTURE	PRAYER	BENEFITS
1. ADMIT your need	Romans 3:23 Romans 6:23	Acknowledge you are a sinner	Eternal life
2. RECOGNIZE the provision	Romans 5:8 Romans 5:19	Acknowledge Christ died on the cross for you	Provides for your needs
3. ACCEPT forgiveness	Acts 3:19 Ephesians 2:8	Say you are sorry for your old ways and receive forgiveness	Eternal forgiveness
4. INVITE Christ into your life	Romans 10:13	Invite Christ into your heart	Continued relationship in prayer with a living God
5. COMMIT your life to Him	1 Peter 1:2 1 Peter 4:19 2 John 1:6 Psalms 37:4-5	Express your willingness to live for Christ, ask for His help to grow in your knowledge and understanding of Him and His will for your life	Obedience and a disciplined life with Christ will carry over to your personal and work life

DATE OF YOUR SPIRITUAL BIRTHDAY_____

GOD'S GIFTS TO YOU	SCRIPTURE	PRAYER	BENEFITS
HOLY SPIRIT	John 14:14-18, 26 Hebrews 13:6 1 Corinthians 12:4 Matthew 7:11 Galatians 5:22	Thank God for the gift of the Spirit	Comforter Helper Giver of Gifts Fruit of the Spirit
HIS PROMISES	2 Peter 1:3-4 2 Corinthians 12:9 Isaiah 40:31 James 1:5-8 1 John 1:7 Psalms 121:7-8 Isaiah 26:3-4	Ask Christ to reveal all things that are good and pure Give thanks for this special day	Security Power Strength Wisdom Fellowship Preservation Peace